To Tier,
a dear aunt and courageous survivor

—*M. B.*

To the struggling species and the
ever shrinking habitats that support them

—*B. J. D.*

Published by
PEACHTREE PUBLISHERS, LTD.
1700 Chattahoochee Avenue
Atlanta, Georgia 30318-2112

www.peachtree-online.com

Manufactured in China

Book design by Loraine M. Joyner
Composition by Melanie M. McMahon

10 9 8 7 6 5 4 3 2

Library of Congress Cataloging-in-Publication Data
Batten, Mary.
  Aliens from Earth / written by Mary Batten ; illustrated by Beverly Doyle.-- 1st ed.
      p. cm.
Summary: Explores how and why plants and animals enter ecosystems to which they are not native, as well
as the consequences of these invasions for other animals, plants, and humans.
  ISBN 1-56145-236-X
  1. Biological invasions--Juvenile literature. [1. Animal introduction. 2. Plant introduction.] I. Doyle,
Beverly, 1963- ill. II. Title.
  QH353 .B29 2003
  577'.18--dc21
                          2002013170

Aliens from Earth

When Animals and Plants Invade Other Ecosystems

Written by Mary Batten
Illustrated by Beverly J. Doyle

PEACHTREE
ATLANTA

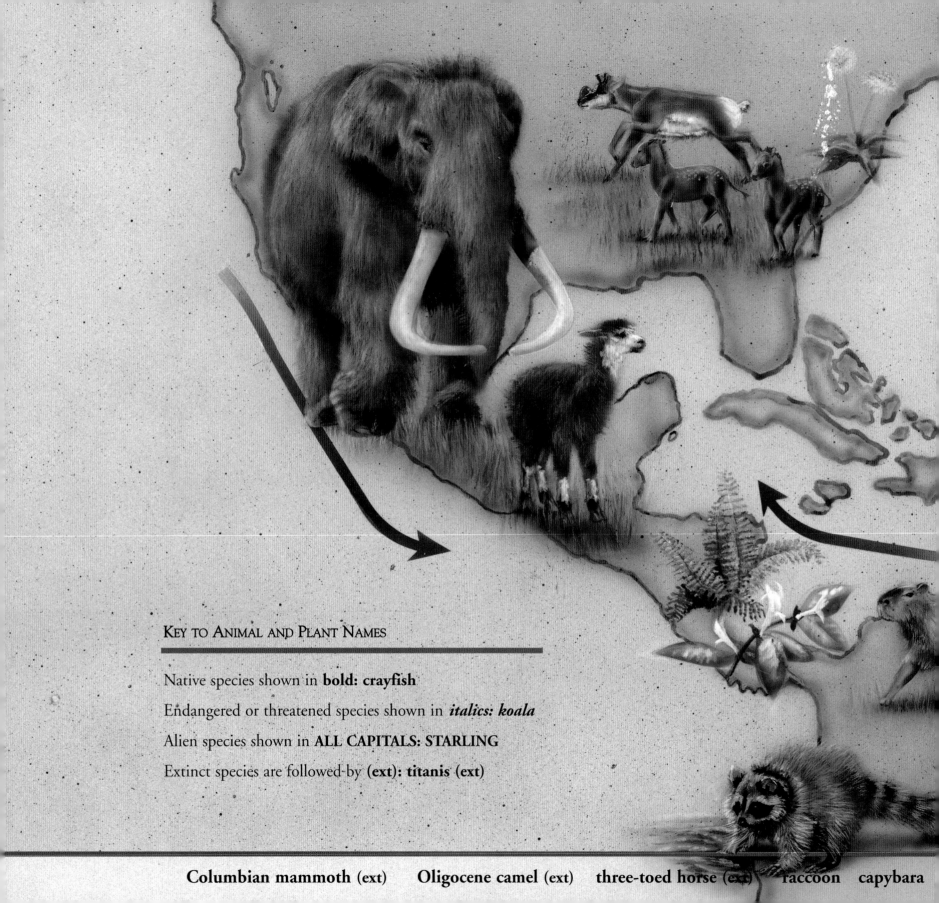

KEY TO ANIMAL AND PLANT NAMES

Native species shown in **bold: crayfish**

Endangered or threatened species shown in *italics: koala*

Alien species shown in **ALL CAPITALS: STARLING**

Extinct species are followed by **(ext): titanis (ext)**

Columbian mammoth (ext)   **Oligocene camel** (ext)   **three-toed horse** (ext)   **raccoon**   **capybara**

ALIENS ARE EVERYWHERE. These are not creatures from other planets, but real living things right here on Earth. Aliens are plants or animals that invade another ecosystem—a natural community of plants and animals living in balance with one another. Scientists call these aliens exotics, a word that means "to come from outside."

A healthy ecosystem needs biodiversity (a variety of living organisms) and a balance between predators and prey. Alien invaders can upset the balance of an ecosystem and threaten its biodiversity.

For millions of years, living things traveled from one place to another, but never so quickly as today. Throughout most of Earth's long evolutionary history, animals walked, flew, and crawled across ancient land bridges from one continent to another. Carried by wind, water, birds, and other animals, seeds moved from place to place. Over thousands of centuries, ecosystems changed, some species became extinct, and new ones evolved, but the pace was slow.

opossum   **giant sloth** (ext)   **glyptodon** (ext)   **titanis** (ext)

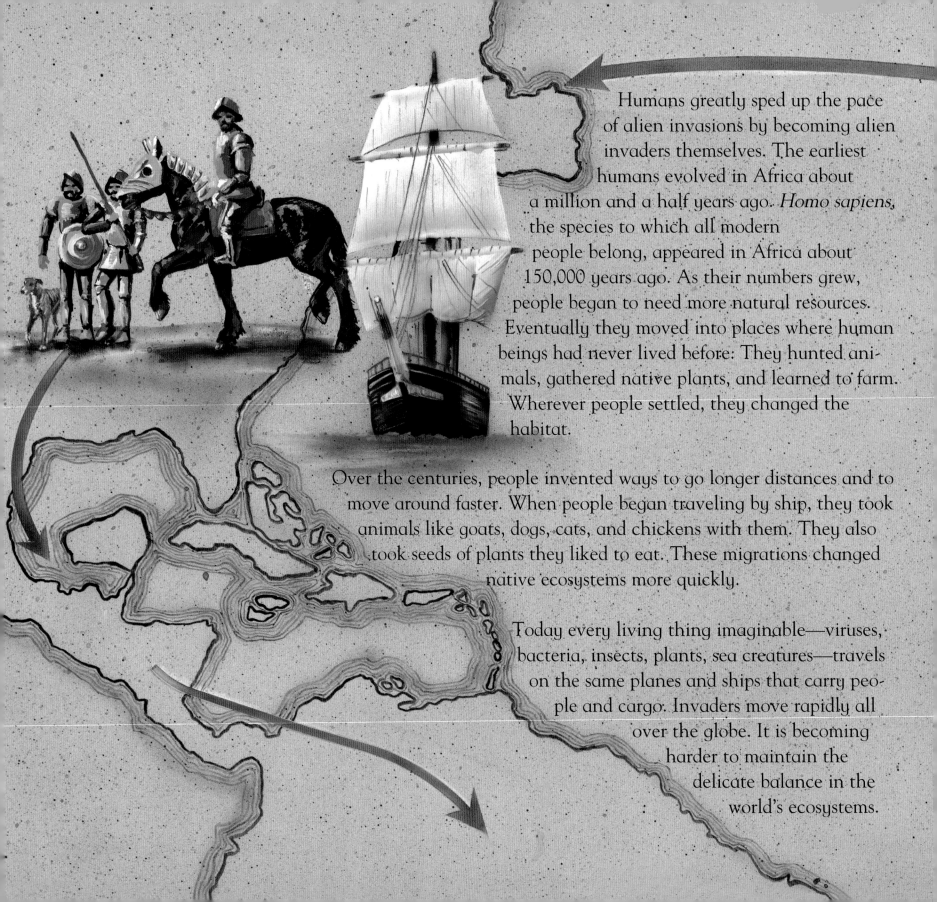

Humans greatly sped up the pace of alien invasions by becoming alien invaders themselves. The earliest humans evolved in Africa about a million and a half years ago. *Homo sapiens*, the species to which all modern people belong, appeared in Africa about 150,000 years ago. As their numbers grew, people began to need more natural resources. Eventually they moved into places where human beings had never lived before. They hunted animals, gathered native plants, and learned to farm. Wherever people settled, they changed the habitat.

Over the centuries, people invented ways to go longer distances and to move around faster. When people began traveling by ship, they took animals like goats, dogs, cats, and chickens with them. They also took seeds of plants they liked to eat. These migrations changed native ecosystems more quickly.

Today every living thing imaginable—viruses, bacteria, insects, plants, sea creatures—travels on the same planes and ships that carry people and cargo. Invaders move rapidly all over the globe. It is becoming harder to maintain the delicate balance in the world's ecosystems.

ISLANDS ARE ESPECIALLY VULNERABLE TO ALIENS. Because islands are surrounded by water, they are cut off from other lands. Their native species have evolved in isolation and often have not developed defenses to protect them from aliens. Until very recently in Earth's history, few new species were able to cross the miles of ocean to reach distant islands, but today every ship or plane that goes to an island may carry an alien invader.

Even a large island continent like Australia can suffer damage from such alien invasions.

DOMESTIC SHEEP AND CATTLE   **FOX**   *numbat*

koala and cub   thylacine (ext)   DOMESTIC CAT   *banded hare wallaby*   CANE TOAD

ALIEN INVASIONS OCCUR IN VARIOUS WAYS. When people migrated to new lands, they sometimes took alien species with them. About 200 years ago, Europeans who colonized Australia took rabbits, foxes, and other animals to hunt. They also took cats to rid the fields of rats that had arrived as stowaways on settlers' ships. Because these recent arrivals encountered no predators, they multiplied quickly, took over more than their share of space and food, and threatened the survival of the native animals. As the numbers of these aliens increased, biodiversity decreased. The cats, for example, escaped into the wild. Without natural enemies, they grew big and fierce. The cats and foxes feasted on some of Australia's unique marsupials and ate them into extinction.

burrowing bettong   FOX

Without natural predators, the rabbit population also exploded. Today Australia has more than 500 million rabbits. Troublesome pests, they destroy soil, damage farmers' crops, and wreck the habitat of many native species.

bridled nail tail wallaby   RABBIT   *Australian mala*   glider   *bilby*   DOMESTIC CAT

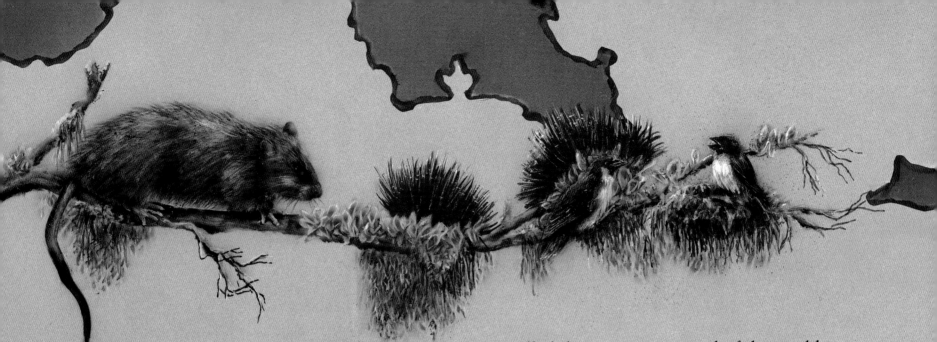

Hawaii, a state made up of islands, has been called the invasion capital of the world. Approximately five new plants and twenty alien species of insects are accidentally introduced there every year.

European domestic pigs were among the earliest aliens introduced to Hawaii. Well suited to life in the islands' wet forests, their population grew rapidly. The pigs dug at the starchy roots of native tree ferns and left behind hollow spots that collected rainwater. No one suspected that these little fern ponds would one day become a perfect habitat for mosquitoes, an insect that did not inhabit Hawaii at that time.

In 1826, when sailors from the whaling ship *Wellington* rinsed out their water barrels, they unknowingly dumped mosquito larvae into the fern ponds. The mosquitoes bred there quickly. These insects carried a blood parasite that caused malaria in native birds, killing off several species. Many kinds of honeycreepers, Hawaii's most famous birds, are now extinct. Partly because of the introduction of so many alien species such as cats and mongooses, and partly because of the destruction of rainforest habitat, the extinction rate of Hawaii's birds is the highest in the United States—and one of the highest in the world.

BROWN RAT   *po'ouli*

DOMESTIC PIG   **MONGOOSE**   *'i'iwi*   **MOSQUITO**

YOU DON'T HAVE TO LIVE ON AN ISLAND to see an alien. You may find one in your own backyard.

Although they have made themselves at home, starlings were once aliens in North America. In the 1890s, a group of people in New York decided to import all the birds mentioned in Shakespeare's plays. They brought in a few pairs of starlings along with the other birds and released them in New York's Central Park. The people did not realize the problems the starlings might cause. These aggressive birds compete with native birds for food and take over the nests of some species. There are now about 200 million starlings throughout the United States.

STARLING

A NOTHER HUMAN MISJUDGMENT brought about the invasion of the gypsy moth.

Étienne Trouvelot, a French scientist who lived in Massachusetts, brought the first gypsy moths from Europe into the United States in 1869. He hoped to use them to breed a new kind of silkworm. Some of the gypsy moths escaped. Without many predators, the moth population exploded. In its caterpillar stage, the moth eats the leaves from trees. Just twenty years after they were introduced in the U.S., gypsy moth caterpillars began damaging New England forests. Since 1980, the gypsy moth has destroyed almost a million acres of forests in the Northeast each year. It has now spread to many other states.

GYPSY MOTH   **GYPSY MOTH EGG SAC**

It is easy for the gypsy moth to travel. Its eggs can be transported on cars, firewood, lawn furniture, tents, backpacks, or anything that is used outdoors—even the soles of people's boots.

GYPSY MOTH LARVAE SUSPENDED ON SILK THREADS   GYPSY MOTH CATERPILLAR

SOME ALIEN SPECIES were introduced entirely by accident.

Exotic fire ants came from South America, arriving by cargo ship at the port of Mobile, Alabama, in the late 1930s. Without any predators, their population grew quickly. These destructive aliens cause billions of dollars in damage each year. They can ruin air conditioners and electrical equipment, and they can damage fifty kinds of crops, including corn and soybeans.

FIRE ANT

white-footed field mouse

The burning sting of the fire ant can blind and even kill young livestock and wildlife. Fire ants have displaced two native ant species. They have now invaded ten southern states and spread as far west as California.

FIRE ANT   swallow

SOMETIMES SCIENTISTS IMPORT AN ALIEN SPECIES for research, and then an accident occurs. This is what happened with the Africanized honeybee, often called the killer bee. In 1956, hoping to improve the breeding stock of honeybees for Brazilian beekeepers, a scientist imported some African bee queens to Brazil. Because worker bees do not fly away as long as the queen remains within the hive, the scientist installed screens to keep the queens inside. But when a local beekeeper innocently removed the screens, twenty-six queens flew away into the forest, and the swarms of worker bees followed them.

AFRICANIZED BEE

The scientist thought that the African bees would die in the forest, but instead they bred with local honeybees. The offspring, which look much like other honeybees, are called Africanized honeybees. These exotic bees defend their hives more fiercely than other honeybees, so they have caused some serious problems. The Africanized bees have stung some farm animals and even a few people to death. They have continued to interbreed with local honeybees as they spread northward into Central America and the United States.

AFRICANIZED BEES

leopard frog   ZEBRA MUSSEL   ZEBRA MUSSELS attached to freshwater mussels   freshwater minnow

MANY ALIENS ARRIVE in the ballast tanks on cargo ships. These large tanks of seawater, which help ships stay balanced, are like aquariums in the middle of the ship. When a ship arrives in port, it dumps its ballast tank, emptying thousands of sea urchins, worms, clams, snails, and other creatures into an ecosystem where they do not belong.

This is how zebra mussels traveled from Europe to the United States. Since arriving on cargo ships in the late 1980s, the zebra mussel has spread throughout the Great Lakes and to many lakes and rivers beyond. Huge populations of these mussels live on submerged rocks, concrete, wood, and metal. They sink buoys, clog water-intake pipes, and eat the plankton on which local fish depend. There are so many zebra mussels that it is impossible to get rid of them. The United States now has rules to control the dumping of ballast water.

crayfish

CAULERPA IS A TYPE OF ALGAE originally grown as an aquarium plant. Some people think it entered ocean waters when the Oceanographic Museum of Monaco dumped some of its algae into the Mediterranean Sea in 1984. By 1999, the algae had spread like a thick green carpet over more than 10,000 acres of Mediterranean seabed.

Caulerpa smothers sea plants and animals and releases a poison that destroys the eggs of many small fishes. The algae grow rapidly. Even a tiny piece can bud into an entire new plant. Caulerpa can live for ten days out of water, float back into the ocean on a high tide, and continue to grow.

monk seal

CAULERPA BED

Caulerpa has already destroyed sea life in some parts of the Mediterranean seabed. Recently it has been found in two sites in southern California.

monk seal

pilot whale

WHEN PEOPLE INTRODUCED KUDZU to the United States, they had good intentions. Kudzu is a fast-growing green vine. The Japanese brought kudzu into the United States to decorate their exhibit at the 1876 Centennial Exposition in Philadelphia, Pennsylvania. Americans liked the beautiful vine with its sweet-smelling blossoms and began planting it in their gardens.

In the 1930s, the U.S. government, hoping to save some of the farmland that was being lost to erosion, hired hundreds of workers to plant kudzu. People believed that the vine would help to prevent soil from being washed away during rains.

DOMESTIC CATTLE

No one realized that the warm, humid climate of the southeastern states was more suitable for kudzu than that of its native Japan. Today this vine, which can grow up to a foot a day, covers some seven million acres in the deep South. It severely damages forests by covering trees and preventing them from getting sunlight.

KUDZU

SOMETIMES WELL-MEANING PEOPLE import an alien species to get rid of a local pest. But that can end up creating a much bigger problem.

In the 1930s, beetles were damaging sugarcane fields in the United States, Australia, and other countries. People imported cane toads—large, insect-eating amphibians that can weigh up to four pounds—from South America to eat the beetles. But things didn't go as expected. The toads ignored the beetles and ate human garbage and pet food instead. The poison secreted from special glands on the toads' shoulders killed dogs and cats that tried to eat them.

DINGO   CANE TOAD

Another similar experiment of the 1930s also ended in failure. To bring a growing population of rats under control, farmers from the Marshall Islands brought in giant monitor lizards. Because the two species weren't active at the same time—rats are nighttime animals and monitor lizards are daytime creatures—they didn't encounter one another. Rather than eating the rats, the lizards ate the islanders' chickens. Then, in an effort to control the lizards, the islanders imported the cane toad. The toads seemed to control the lizards, but then the toad population increased, leading to the deaths of cats and dogs, animals that had been fairly effective in keeping the rats in check. In the end, the farmers were worse off than they had been before the start of the experiment.

GIANT MONITOR LIZARD   **CANE TOAD   YOUNG GIANT MONITOR LIZARD**

SOME PEOPLE ILLEGALLY CARRY exotic animals across borders to sell or to keep as pets. Customs officials have found iguanas, electric eels, snapping turtles, hamsters, parrots, and other animals in luggage, shoe boxes, and plastic bowls. Smuggling exotic animals not only introduces aliens into a new habitat but also may deplete the native populations of certain species.

IGUANA   PAINTED TURTLE

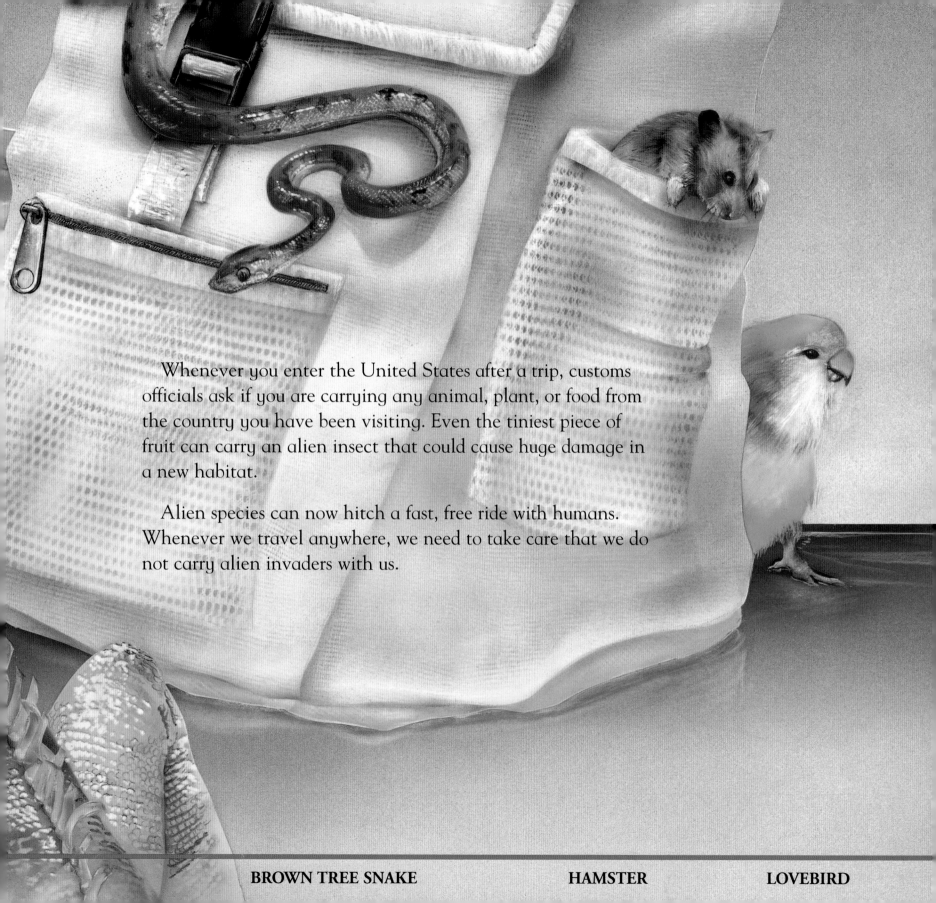

Whenever you enter the United States after a trip, customs officials ask if you are carrying any animal, plant, or food from the country you have been visiting. Even the tiniest piece of fruit can carry an alien insect that could cause huge damage in a new habitat.

Alien species can now hitch a fast, free ride with humans. Whenever we travel anywhere, we need to take care that we do not carry alien invaders with us.

BROWN TREE SNAKE   **HAMSTER**   **LOVEBIRD**

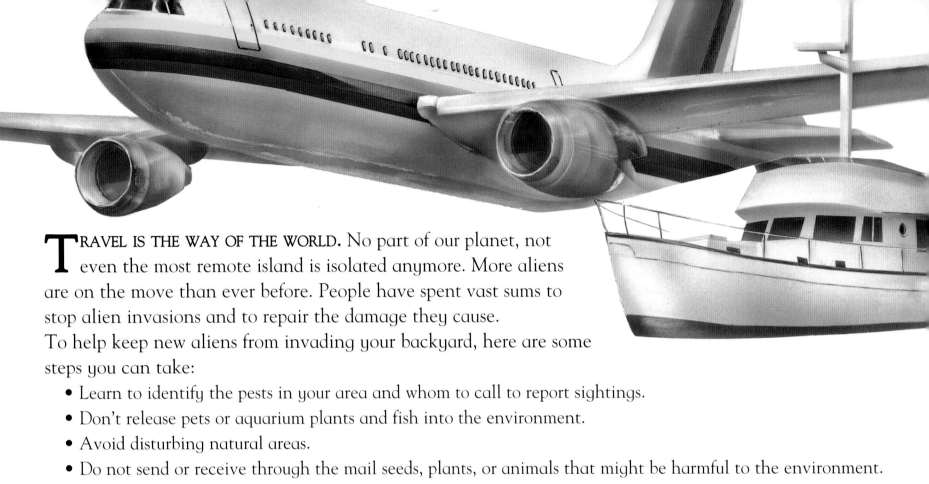

Travel is the way of the world. No part of our planet, not even the most remote island is isolated anymore. More aliens are on the move than ever before. People have spent vast sums to stop alien invasions and to repair the damage they cause.

To help keep new aliens from invading your backyard, here are some steps you can take:

- Learn to identify the pests in your area and whom to call to report sightings.
- Don't release pets or aquarium plants and fish into the environment.
- Avoid disturbing natural areas.
- Do not send or receive through the mail seeds, plants, or animals that might be harmful to the environment.
- When you and your family travel, do not bring plants, fruits, soil, seeds, or animals into your country from abroad.
- Clean your boats and boating equipment before taking them from one body of water to another. Leave behind any unused bait and bucket water.
- Clean your boots and camping gear before going to another area or country, and again before returning home.
- Learn more about invasive species by reading books and articles and by checking websites like www.invasivespecies.gov.

The place where you live is your habitat. You share it with many different kinds of animals and plants. Help protect them, yourself, and Earth's biodiversity from alien invaders.

GLOSSARY

biodiversity: The variety of different plants and animals and ecosystems that make up life on Earth.

community: All the organisms—animals, plants, and microorganisms—that live together in a particular place, such as a forest or a seashore.

ecosystem: A community of plants and animals living in balance with each other and with their environment. An ecosystem can be small like a pond or large like the ocean or the entire planet.

endangered species: A group of animals or plants that are at risk of extinction (according to the Endangered Species Act of 1973).

environment: The surroundings and conditions—including water, light, soil, food sources, and other organisms—that affect the growth and development of living things.

extinct: No longer existing in living form.

habitat: The particular environment where a plant or animal normally lives and grows.

migration: The long-distance movement of living things from one region to another.

organism: Any living thing.

parasite: An organism that lives in or on a different organism, called a host, from which it gets food. Parasites are often harmful to the host.

population: All the organisms of a species living in a certain area.

predator: An animal that lives by hunting and feeding upon other animals.

prey: Animals that are hunted and eaten by other animals.

species: A group of closely related animals or plants that can breed with one another in nature.

threatened species: A group of animals or plants that are at risk of becoming endangered (according to the Endangered Species Act of 1973).